YO-BUY-089

American Governors and Gubernatorial Elections 1979-1987

American Governors
and
Gubernatorial Elections
1979-1987

Compiled by
Marie Marmo Mullaney

MECKLER

Library of Congress Cataloging-in-Publication Data

Mullaney, Marie Marmo.
   American governors and gubernatorial elections, 1979-1987 /
  compiled by Marie Marmo Mullaney.
    p. cm.
  Updated ed. of: American governors and gubernatorial elections,
1775-1978 / compiled by Roy R. Glashan. c1979.
   Bibliography: p.
   ISBN 0-88736-316-4
   1. Governors--United States--Election--Statistics. 2. Elections--
-United States--States--Statistics. I. Glashan, Roy, R., 1928-
American governors and gubernatorial elections, 1775-1978.
II. Title.
JK2447. M85 1988
353.9'131--dc19   88-13248
                                         CIP

British Cataloguing in Publication Data

Mullaney, Marie Marmo
   American governors and gubernatorial
   elections, 1979-1987.
   1. United States. Governors. Elections,
   1979-1987
   I. Title
   324.973
   ISBN 0-88736-316-4

Meckler Corporation, 11 Ferry Lane West, Westport, CT 06880.
Meckler Ltd, Grosvenor Gardens House, Grosvenor Gardens,
  London SW1W 0BS, UK.

Printed on acid free paper.
Manufactured in the United States of America.

Contents

Introduction

This new volume of *American Governors and Gubernatorial Elections*, bringing coverage from 1979 up through 1987[1], should serve as a valuable research and reference aid for those seeking basic biographical information about American governors, and students wishing to do statistical analysis of voting trends in state gubernatorial elections. Statistics, however, do not tell the whole story. Readers are encouraged to search out more information about the personalities and campaigns detailed here.

This present cohort of chief executives includes within it visible testimony of the changing demographic face of American politics: John Waihee, the first Hawaiian governor of native Hawaiian ancestry; Toney Anaya of New Mexico and Bob Martinez of Florida, representative of the growing regional clout of Hispanic-Americans; a handful of women — Madeline Kunin of Vermont, Vesta Roy of New Hampshire, Kay Orr of Nebraska, Ella Grasso of Connecticut, Dixy Lee Ray of Washington, Martha Layne Collins of Kentucky. While these examples are few, they may be indicative of future trends, or at the very least should serve to alert observers to forces on the political horizon.

Note that in 1986 Nebraska, a conservative but populist farm state, became the first to nominate women as gubernatorial candidates of both major political parties. While black Americans are still waiting to break the color barrier that has kept them from state executive mansions in the twentieth century, recent campaigns have seen historic breakthroughs. Thomas Bradley, the mayor of Los Angeles, came very close to achieving his dream of becoming the nation's first elected black governor in the California campaigns of both 1982 and 1986, while in 1986 Bill Lucas of Michigan became not only the first black to win the Republican nomination for governor in Michigan, but also the first black since Reconstruction to win the GOP nomination for governor anywhere.

The story of the "New Politics" in the New South is another that bears close watching. Bill Clements of Texas and Guy Hunt of Alabama became the first Republican governors of their respective states in this century, while Florida's Bob Martinez, North Carolina's Jim Martin, and South Carolina's Carroll Campbell became the second.

Finally, as the 1988 presidential election year unfolds, we are reminded once again of the path from state house to White House. Contenders for their party's Presidential nomination in 1988 have included Governor Michael Dukakis of

---

1. See Glashan, Roy, compiler. *American Governors and Gubernatorial Elections, 1775-1978.* Westport, CT: Meckler, 1979

Massachusetts and former Governors Pete DuPont of Delaware and Bruce Babbitt of Arizona. The Vice-Presidential prospects have included, among others, Governor Tom Kean of New Jersey and former Governor Charles Robb of Virginia.

All in all, the study of state gubernatorial politics makes for a fascinating education in the American electoral process.

Marie Marmo Mullaney
Caldwell College
Caldwell, New Jersey

American Governors
and Gubernatorial Elections,
1979-1987

2 American Governors

ALABAMA GOVERNORS

STATE OF ALABAMA

GOVERNOR	BIRTH DATE	BIRTHPLACE	BECAME GOV.	AGE
(FORREST) "FOB" JAMES Jr.	9-15-1934	Lanett, Alab.....	1-15-1979	44
GEORGE C. WALLACE Jr.....	8-25-1919	Clio, Alab.......	1-17-1983	63
(HAROLD) GUY HUNT........	6-17-1933	Holly Pond, Alab.	1-19-1987	53

ALABAMA GUBERNATORIAL ELECTIONS

STATE OF ALABAMA

DATE	DEMOCRATIC VOTE		REPUBLICAN VOTE	
11-7-1978	F.JAMES Jr......551,886	72.6%	G. Hunt.........196,963	25.9%
11-2-1982	G.WALLACE Jr....650,538	57.6%	E. Folmar.......440,815	39.1%
11-4-1986	B. Baxley.......530,051	44.0%	G. HUNT.........687,832	56.0%

PARTY	MAJOR OCCUPATIONS	ALABAMA RESIDENCE	DEATH DATE AGE
Dem	businessman.........	Opelika....................	
Dem	lawyer, judge.......	Montgomery...............	
Rep	farmer.............	Holly Pond...............	

DATE	OTHER SIGNIFICANT VOTE		SCATTERED VOTE	
11-7-1978	....	.....	11,625	1.5%
11-2-1982	....	.....	37,242	3.3%
11-4-1986	....	.....	....	....

4 American Governors

ALASKA GOVERNORS

STATE OF ALASKA

GOVERNOR	BIRTH DATE	BIRTHPLACE	BECAME GOV.	AGE
JAY S. HAMMOND...........7-21-1922		Troy, N.Y.......	12-2-1974	52
WILLIAM J. SHEFFIELD.....6-26-1928		Spokane, Wash...	12-6-1982	54
STEVE COWPER.............8-21-1938		Petersburg, Va..	12-1-1986	48

ALASKA GUBERNATORIAL ELECTIONS

STATE OF ALASKA

DATE	DEMOCRATIC VOTE		REPUBLICAN VOTE	
11-7-1978	C. Croft.........25,656	20.2%	J. HAMMOND.......49,580	39.1%
11-2-1982	W.J.SHEFFIELD....89,918	46.1%	Tom A. Fink......72,291	37.1%
11-4-1986	S.COWPER.........84,943	48.9%	A. Sturgulewski..76,515	43.9%

PARTY	MAJOR OCCUPATIONS	ALASKA RESIDENCE	DEATH DATE AGE
Rep	guide, resort owner..	South Naknek...............	
Dem	broadcaster, engineer	Anchorage..................	
Dem	lawyer..............	Fairbanks..................	

DATE	OTHER SIGNIFICANT VOTE		SCATTERED VOTE	
11-7-1978	W. Hickel.....WI..33,555	26.4%	18,119	14.3%
11-2-1982	R. Randolph....L..29,067	14.9%	3,609	1.9%
11-4-1986	J. Vogler....AMI..10,013	5.7%	3,019	1.5%

WI = write-in votes   L = Libertarian

AMI = American Independent

6 American Governors

ARIZONA GOVERNORS

STATE OF ARIZONA

GOVERNOR	BIRTH DATE	BIRTHPLACE	BECAME GOV.	AGE
BRUCE E. BABBITT.........6-27-1938		Flagstaff, Ariz..	1-1-1979	40
EVAN MECHAM..............5-12-1924		Duchesne, Utah...	1-5-1987	62

ARIZONA GUBERNATORIAL ELECTIONS

STATE OF ARIZONA

DATE	DEMOCRATIC VOTE		REPUBLICAN VOTE	
11-7-1978	B.BABBITT.......282,605	52.5%	E. Mecham.......241,093	44.8%
11-2-1982	B.BABBITT.......453,795	62.5%	L. Corbet.......235,877	32.5%
11-4-1986	C. Warner.......293,944	34.0%	E. MECHAM.......339,773	40.0%

PARTY	MAJOR OCCUPATIONS	ARIZONA RESIDENCE	DEATH DATE AGE
Dem	lawyer...............	Phoenix......................	
Rep	car dealer, publisher	Glendale....................	

DATE	OTHER SIGNIFICANT VOTE		SCATTERED VOTE	
11-7-1978	....	.....	14,858	2.7%
11-2-1982	Sam Steiger.......L...36,649	5.0%	....	.....
11-4-1986	B.Schulz..........I..221,633	26.0%	....	.....

L = Libertarian   I = Independent

ARKANSAS GOVERNORS

STATE OF ARKANSAS

GOVERNOR	BIRTH DATE	BIRTHPLACE	BECAME GOV.	AGE
WILLIAM J. (BILL) CLINTON	8-19-1946	Hope, Ark........	1-9-1979	32
FRANK D. WHITE...........	6-4-1933	Texarkana, Ark...	1-19-1981	47
WILLIAM J. (BILL) CLINTON	8-19-1946	Hope, Ark........	1-11-1983	36

ARKANSAS GUBERNATORIAL ELECTIONS

STATE OF ARKANSAS

DATE	DEMOCRATIC VOTE		REPUBLICAN VOTE	
11-7-1978	W. CLINTON......331,611	63.3%	A. Lowe.........192,256	36.7%
11-4-1980	W. Clinton......403,241	48.1%	F. WHITE........435,684	51.9%
11-2-1982	W. CLINTON......431,855	54.7%	F. White........357,496	45.3%
11-6-1984	W. CLINTON......554,561	62.6%	W. Freeman......331,987	37.4%
11-4-1986	W. CLINTON......425,372	64.0%	F. White........240,464	36.0%

PARTY	MAJOR OCCUPATIONS	ARKANSAS RESIDENCE	DEATH DATE	AGE
Dem	lawyer...............	Fayetteville.................		
Rep	banker...............	Little Rock..................		
Dem	lawyer...............	Little Rock..................		

DATE	OTHER SIGNIFICANT VOTE		SCATTERED VOTE	
11-7-1978	....	.....	65	0.0%
11-4-1980	....	.....	....	.....
11-2-1982	....	.....	....	.....
11-6-1984	....	.....	....	.....
11-4-1986	....	.....	....	.....

CALIFORNIA GOVERNORS

STATE OF CALIFORNIA

GOVERNOR	BIRTH DATE	BIRTHPLACE	BECAME GOV.	AGE
(EDMUND G.) JERRY BROWN Jr.	4-7-1938	San Francisco, Ca.	1-6-1975	36
GEORGE DEUKMEJIAN..........	6-6-1928	Menands, N.Y......	1-3-1983	54

CALIFORNIA GUBERNATORIAL ELECTIONS

STATE OF CALIFORNIA

DATE	DEMOCRATIC VOTE		REPUBLICAN VOTE	
11-7-1978	E. BROWN Jr...3,835,946	56.1%	E. Younger....2,491,414	36.4%
11-2-1982	T. Bradley....3,787,669	48.1%	G.DEUKMEJIAN..3,881,014	49.3%
11-4-1986	T. Bradley....2,781,714	37.4%	G.DEUKMEJIAN..4,506,601	60.5%

PARTY	MAJOR OCCUPATIONS	CALIFORNIA RESIDENCE	DEATH DATE	AGE
Dem	lawyer...............	Laurel Canyon, Los Angeles...		
Rep	lawyer...............	Long Beach..................		

DATE	OTHER SIGNIFICANT VOTE		SCATTERED VOTE	
11-7-1978	E.Clark...........I..374,047	5.5%	135,996	2.0%
11-2-1982	....	.....	207,652	2.6%
11-4-1986	....	.....	155,170	2.1%

I = Independent

COLORADO GOVERNORS

STATE OF COLORADO				
GOVERNOR	BIRTH DATE	BIRTHPLACE	BECAME GOV.	AGE
RICHARD D. LAMM........	8-3-1935	Madison, Wis.....	1-14-1975	39
ROY ROMER..............	10-31-1928	Garden City, Kan.	1-13-1987	58

COLORADO GUBERNATORIAL ELECTIONS

STATE OF COLORADO			
DATE	DEMOCRATIC VOTE	REPUBLICAN VOTE	
11-7-1978	R. LAMM........483,984 58.8%	T. Strickland...317,292	38.5%
11-2-1982	R. LAMM........627,960 65.7%	J. Fuhr.........302,740	31.7%
11-4-1986	R. ROMER.......616,325 58.2%	T. Strickland...434,420	41.0%

PARTY	MAJOR OCCUPATIONS	COLORADO RESIDENCE	DEATH DATE	AGE
Dem	lawyer, professor....	Denver......................		
Dem	lawyer, businessman..	Denver......................		

DATE	OTHER SIGNIFICANT VOTE		SCATTERED VOTE	
11-7-1978	....	.....	22,530	2.7%
11-2-1982	....	.....	25,321	2.6%
11-4-1986	....	.....	8,183	0.8%

CONNECTICUT GOVERNORS

STATE OF CONNECTICUT

GOVERNOR	BIRTH DATE	BIRTHPLACE	BECAME GOV.	AGE
ELLA (TAMBUSSI) GRASSO.a	5-10-1919	Windsor Locks, Conn	1-8-1975	55
WILLIAM A. O'NEILL......	8-11-1930	Hartford, Conn.....	12-31-1980	50

a Resigned; succeeded by the lieutenant governor

CONNECTICUT GUBERNATORIAL ELECTIONS

STATE OF CONNECTICUT

DATE	DEMOCRATIC VOTE		REPUBLICAN VOTE	
11-7-1978	E. GRASSO.......613,109	59.1%	R. Sarasin......422,316	40.8%
11-2-1982	W. O'NEILL......578,264	53.3%	L. Rome.........497,773	45.9%
11-4-1986	W. O'NEILL......575,638	57.9%	J. Belaga.......408,489	41.1%

PARTY	MAJOR OCCUPATIONS	CONNECTICUT RESIDENCE	DEATH DATE	AGE
Dem	government service...	Windsor Locks................	2-5-1981	61
Dem	insurance agent......	East Hampton................		

DATE	OTHER SIGNIFICANT VOTE		SCATTERED VOTE	
11-7-1978	....	.....	1,183	0.1%
11-2-1982	....	.....	7,839	0.8%
11-4-1986	....	.....	9,565	1.0%

DELAWARE GOVERNORS

STATE OF DELAWARE

GOVERNOR	BIRTH DATE	BIRTHPLACE	BECAME GOV.	AGE
PIERRE S. DuPONT 4th....	1-22-1935	Wilmington, Del..	1-18-1977	41
MICHAEL N. CASTLE.......	7-2-1939	Wilmington, Del..	1-15-1985	45

DELAWARE GUBERNATORIAL ELECTIONS

STATE OF DELAWARE

DATE	DEMOCRATIC VOTE		REPUBLICAN VOTE	
11-2-1976	S. Tribbitt......97,480	42.5%	P. DuPONT 4th...130,531	56.8%
11-4-1980	W. Gordy.........64,217	29.0%	P. DuPONT 4th...159,004	71.0%
11-6-1984	w. Quillen......108,315	44.5%	M. CASTLE.......132,250	55.5%

PARTY	MAJOR OCCUPATIONS	DELAWARE RESIDENCE	DEATH DATE AGE
Rep	business executive...	Wilmington..................	
Rep	lawyer..............	Wilmington..................	

DATE	OTHER SIGNIFICANT VOTE		SCATTERED VOTE	
11-2-1976	....	.....	1,552	0.7%
11-4-1980	....	......	....	.....
11-6-1984	....	......	....	.....

FLORIDA GOVERNORS

STATE OF FLORIDA

GOVERNOR	BIRTH DATE	BIRTHPLACE	BECAME GOV.	AGE
(DANIEL) ROBERT GRAHAM.a	11-9-1936	Coral Gables, Fla	1-2-1979	39
JOHN WAYNE MIXSON......b	6-17-1922	Coffee Co, Ala...	1-3-1987	64
ROBERT ("BOB") MARTINEZ.	12-25-1934	Tampa, Fla.......	1-6-1987	52

a Resigned; succeeded by the lieutenant governor

b Became Florida's 39th governor for a three-day period when Governor
  Bob Graham resigned three days early to become the state's junior
  U.S. Senator. Governor-elect Bob Martinez was sworn in as Florida's
  40th governor on 1-6-1987.

FLORIDA GUBERNATORIAL ELECTIONS

STATE OF FLORIDA

DATE	DEMOCRATIC VOTE		REPUBLICAN VOTE	
11-7-1978	R. GRAHAM.....1,406,580	55.6%	J. Eckerd.....1,123,888	44.4%
11-2-1982	R. GRAHAM.....1,739,553	64.7%	L. Bafalis......949,013	35.3%
11-4-1986	S. Pajcic.....1,489,272	46.0%	R. MARTINEZ...1,767,971	54.0%

PARTY	MAJOR OCCUPATIONS	FLORIDA RESIDENCE	DEATH DATE AGE
Dem	lawyer, farmer.......	Miami Lakes..................	
Dem	cattle rancher.......	Tallahassee..................	
Rep	teacher, consultant..	Tampa.......................	

DATE	OTHER SIGNIFICANT VOTE		SCATTERED VOTE	
11-7-1978	....	.....	....	.....
11-2-1982	....	.....	....	.....
11-4-1986	....	.....	....	.....

GEORGIA GOVERNORS

STATE OF GEORGIA

GOVERNOR	BIRTH DATE	BIRTHPLACE	BECAME GOV.	AGE
GEORGE D. BUSBEE........	8-7-1927	Vienna, Ga.......	1-14-1975	47
JOE FRANK HARRIS........	2-16-1936	Atco, Ga.........	1-11-1983	46

GEORGIA GUBERNATORIAL ELECTIONS

STATE OF GEORGIA

DATE	DEMOCRATIC VOTE		REPUBLICAN VOTE	
11-7-1978	G. BUSBEE.......534,572	80.7%	R. Cook.........128,139	19.3%
11-2-1982	J. HARRIS.......734,090	62.8%	R. Bell.........434,496	37.2%
11-4-1986	J. HARRIS.......821,957	70.0%	G. Davis........347,556	30.0%

PARTY	MAJOR OCCUPATIONS	GEORGIA RESIDENCE	DEATH DATE AGE
Dem	lawyer...............	Albany.......................	
Dem	concrete business....	Cartersville................	

DATE	OTHER SIGNIFICANT VOTE	SCATTERED VOTE
11-7-1978	....	....
11-2-1982	....	....
11-4-1986	....	....

HAWAII GOVERNORS

STATE OF HAWAII

GOVERNOR	BIRTH DATE	BIRTHPLACE	BECAME GOV.	AGE
GEORGE R. ARIYOSHI......	3-12-1920	Honolulu, Haw....	12-2-1974	54
JOHN WAIHEE............a	5-19-1946	Honokaa, Haw.....	12-1-1986	40

a First governor of native Hawaiian ancestry

HAWAII GUBERNATORIAL ELECTIONS

STATE OF HAWAII

DATE	DEMOCRATIC VOTE		REPUBLICAN VOTE	
11-7-1978	G. ARIYOSHI.....153,394	54.5%	J. Leopold......124,610	44.2%
11-2-1982	G. ARIYOSHI.....141,043	45.2%	D. Anderson......81,507	26.1%
11-4-1986	J. WAIHEE.......165,081	52.0%	D. Anderson.....151,929	48.0%

PARTY	MAJOR OCCUPATIONS	HAWAII RESIDENCE	DEATH DATE	AGE
Dem	lawyer...............	Honolulu.....................		
Dem	lawyer...............	Honolulu.....................		

DATE	OTHER SIGNIFICANT VOTE		SCATTERED VOTE	
11-7-1978	....	.....	3,583	1.3%
11-2-1982	F.F.Fasi..........I...89,303	28.7%	....	.....
11-4-1986	....	......	....	.....

I = Independent

IDAHO GOVERNORS

STATE OF IDAHO

GOVERNOR	BIRTH DATE	BIRTHPLACE	BECAME GOV.	AGE
JOHN V. EVANS...........	1-18-1925	Malad City, Ida..	1-1-1979	53
CECIL D. ANDRUS.........	8-25-1931	Hood River, Ore..	1-5-1987	55

IDAHO GUBERNATORIAL ELECTIONS

STATE OF IDAHO

DATE	DEMOCRATIC VOTE		REPUBLICAN VOTE	
11-7-1978	J. EVANS........169,540	58.8%	A. Larsen.......114,149	39.5%
11-2-1982	J. EVANS........165,365	50.6%	P. Batt.........161,157	49.4%
11-4-1986	C. ANDRUS.......193,429	49.9%	D. Leroy........189,794	49.0%

PARTY	MAJOR OCCUPATIONS	IDAHO RESIDENCE	DEATH DATE	AGE
Dem	rancher, banker......	Malad City...................		
Dem	businessman..........	Boise........................		

DATE	OTHER SIGNIFICANT VOTE		SCATTERED VOTE	
11-7-1978	....	.....	4,877	1.7%
11-2-1982	....	.....	....	.....
11-4-1986	....	.....	4,203	1.1%

ILLINOIS GOVERNORS

STATE OF ILLINOIS

GOVERNOR	BIRTH DATE	BIRTHPLACE	BECAME GOV.	AGE
JAMES R. THOMPSON Jr....	5-8-1936	Chicago, Ill.....	1-10-1977	40

ILLINOIS GUBERNATORIAL ELECTIONS

STATE OF ILLINOIS

DATE	DEMOCRATIC VOTE		REPUBLICAN VOTE	
11-7-1978	M. Bakalis....1,263,134	40.1%	J. THOMPSON...1,859,684	59.0%
11-2-1982	A.Stevenson 1,811,027	49.3%	J. THOMPSON...1,816,101	49.4%
11-4-1986	a............................		J. THOMPSON...1,655,849	52.7%

a Adlai E. Stevenson III, scion of one of Illinois' leading political
  families, rejected the nomination of the Democratic Party when two
  followers of political extremist Lyndon H. LaRouche, Jr. upset his
  running mates in the March 18, 1986 Democratic primary. Rather than
  run on the same ticket with people whose philosophy he opposed, he
  collected nominating petitions to run as head of a new party, Illinois
  Solidarity. No candidate was named by Democratic party authorities
  to replace him.

PARTY	MAJOR OCCUPATIONS	ILLINOIS RESIDENCE	DEATH DATE AGE
Rep	lawyer..............	Chicago.....................	

DATE	OTHER SIGNIFICANT VOTE		SCATTERED VOTE	
11-7-1978	....	.....	27,183	0.9%
11-2-1982	....	.....	46,542	1.3%
11-4-1986	A.E.Stevenson...IS.1,256,626	40.0%	231,503	7.3%

IS = Illinois Solidarity

INDIANA GOVERNORS

STATE OF INDIANA

GOVERNOR	BIRTH DATE	BIRTHPLACE	BECAME GOV.	AGE
OTIS R. BOWEN...........	2-26-1918	Rochester, Ind...	1-8-1973	54
ROBERT ORR..............	11-17-1917	Ann Arbor, Mich..	1-12-1981	63

INDIANA GUBERNATORIAL ELECTIONS

STATE OF INDIANA

DATE	DEMOCRATIC VOTE			REPUBLICAN VOTE		
11-2-1976	L. Conrad.......	927,243	42.6%	O. BOWEN......	1,236,565	56.9%
11-4-1980	J. Hillenbrand..	913,116	41.9%	R. ORR........	1,257,383	57.7%
11-6-1984	W. Townsend...	1,036,922	47.2%	R. ORR........	1,146,497	52.2%

PARTY	MAJOR OCCUPATIONS	INDIANA RESIDENCE	DEATH DATE	AGE
Rep	physician............	Bremen......................		
Rep	businessman..........	Evansville..................		

DATE	OTHER SIGNIFICANT VOTE	SCATTERED VOTE	
11-2-1976	....	11,526	0.5%
11-4-1980	....	............7.904	0.4%
11-6-1984	....	14,569	0.6%

IOWA GOVERNORS

STATE OF IOWA

GOVERNOR	BIRTH DATE	BIRTHPLACE	BECAME GOV.	AGE
ROBERT D. RAY...........	9-26-1929	Des Moines, Iowa.	1-16-1969	39
TERRY E. BRANSTAD.......	11-17-1947	Leland, Iowa.....	1-14-1983	35

IOWA GUBERNATORIAL ELECTIONS

STATE OF IOWA

DATE	DEMOCRATIC VOTE		REPUBLICAN VOTE	
11-7-1978	J. Fitzpatrick..345,519	41.0%	R. RAY.........491,713	58.3%
11-2-1982	R. Conlin.......483,291	46.5%	T. BRANSTAD.....548,313	52.8%
11-4-1986	L. Junkins......436,987	47.9%	T. BRANSTAD.....472,712	52.0%

PARTY	MAJOR OCCUPATIONS	IOWA RESIDENCE	DEATH DATE	AGE
Rep	lawyer...............	Des Moines...................		
Rep	lawyer, farmer.......	Lake Mills...................		

DATE	OTHER SIGNIFICANT VOTE		SCATTERED VOTE	
11-7-1978	....	.....	5,958	0.7%
11-2-1982	....	.....	6,074	0.7%
11-4-1986	....	.....	924	0.1%

KANSAS GOVERNORS

STATE OF KANSAS				
GOVERNOR	BIRTH DATE	BIRTHPLACE	BECAME GOV.	AGE
JOHN W. CARLIN..........	8-3-1940	Salina, Kan......	1-8-1979	38
MIKE HAYDEN.............	3-16-1944	Atwood, Kan......	1-12-1987	42

KANSAS GUBERNATORIAL ELECTIONS

STATE OF KANSAS			
DATE	DEMOCRATIC VOTE	REPUBLICAN VOTE	
11-7-1978	J. CARLIN.......363,835 49.4%	R. Bennett......348,015	47.3%
11-2-1982	J. CARLIN.......405,772 53.2%	S. Hardage......339,356	44.5%
11-4-1986	T. Docking......400,313 48.0%	M. HAYDEN.......431,627	52.0%

PARTY	MAJOR OCCUPATIONS	KANSAS RESIDENCE	DEATH DATE	AGE
Dem	dairy farmer,cattleman	Smolan.....................		
Rep	farmer, biologist.....	Atwood.....................		

DATE	OTHER SIGNIFICANT VOTE		SCATTERED VOTE	
11-7-1978	....	.....	24,396	3.3%
11-2-1982	....	.....	18,135	2.3%
11-4-1986	....	......	....	.....

KENTUCKY GOVERNORS

STATE OF KENTUCKY

GOVERNOR	BIRTH DATE	BIRTHPLACE	BECAME GOV.	AGE
JULIAN M. CARROLL.......	4-16-1931	Paducah, Ky......	12-9-1975	44
JOHN Y. BROWN...........	12-28-1933	Lexington, Ky....	12-11-1979	46
MARTHA LAYNE COLLINS....	12-7-1936	Bagdad, Ky.......	12-13-1983	47
WALLACE G. WILKINSON....	12-12-1941	Liberty, Ky......	12-8-1987	46

KENTUCKY GUBERNATORIAL ELECTIONS

STATE OF KENTUCKY

DATE	DEMOCRATIC VOTE		REPUBLICAN VOTE	
11-4-1975	J. CARROLL......470,159	62.8%	R. Gable........277,998	37.2%
11-6-1979	J. BROWN Jr.....588,088	59.4%	L. Nunn.........381,278	40.6%
11-8-1983	M. COLLINS......561,674	54.6	J. Bunning......454,650	44.2%
11-3-1987	W. WILKINSON....504,674	64.9	J. Harper.......273,141	35.1%

PARTY	MAJOR OCCUPATIONS	KENTUCKY RESIDENCE	DEATH DATE	AGE
Dem	lawyer...............	nr. Paducah................		
Dem	lawyer, businessman..	Lexington....................		
Dem	schoolteacher........	Versailles..................		
Dem	realtor, developer...	Lexington....................		

DATE	OTHER SIGNIFICANT VOTE		SCATTERED VOTE	
11-4-1975	....	......	....	.....
11-6-1979	....	......	....	.....
11-8-1983	....	......	14,347	1.2%
11-3-1987	....	......	....	.....

LOUISIANA GOVERNORS

STATE OF LOUISIANA

GOVERNOR	BIRTH DATE	BIRTHPLACE	BECAME GOV.	AGE
EDWIN W. EDWARDS........	8-7-1927	Marksville, La...	5-9-1972	44
DAVID TREEN.............	7-16-1928	Baton Rouge, La..	3-10-1980	51
EDWIN W. EDWARDS........	8-7-1927	Marksville, La...	3-12-1984	56
(CHARLES) BUDDY ROEMER..	10-4-1943	Shreveport, La...	3-14-1988	43

LOUISIANA GUBERNATORIAL ELECTIONS

STATE OF LOUISIANA

DATE	DEMOCRATIC VOTE		REPUBLICAN VOTE	
12-13-1975	E. EDWARDS......430,095	100.0%	....	.....
12-8-1979	L. Lambert......681,134	49.7%	D. TREEN........690,691	50.3%
10-22-1983	E. EDWARDS....1,006,561	62.3%	D. Treen........588,508	36.4%
10-24-1987	C. ROEMER..a....516,078	33.1%	R. Livingston...287,780	18.5%

a Louisiana holds an open primary election with candidates from all
parties running on the same ballot. Any candidate who receives a
majority is elected. If no candidate receives a majority, there is
a run-off election between the two top finishers. In 1987, incumbent
Edwin Edwards conceded the election after his second-place finish,
foregoing a runoff after two other major challengers indicated they
would support Roemer.

PARTY	MAJOR OCCUPATIONS	LOUISIANA RESIDENCE	DEATH DATE	AGE
Dem	lawyer..............	Crowley......................		
Rep	lawyer..............	Metairie.....................		
Dem	lawyer..............	Crowley......................		
Dem	businessman.........	Bossier City.................		

DATE	OTHER SIGNIFICANT VOTE		SCATTERED VOTE	
12-13-1975	....	.....	....	.....
12-8-1979	....	.....	....	.....
10-22-1983	....	.....	20,836	1.3%
10-24-1987	E.Edwards.........D..437,801	28.1%	24,769	1.6%
	B.Tauzin..........D..154,079	9.9%		
	J.H.Brown.........D..138,223	8.8%		

MAINE GOVERNORS

STATE OF MAINE

GOVERNOR	BIRTH DATE	BIRTHPLACE	BECAME GOV.	AGE
JOSEPH E. BRENNAN.......	11-2-1934	Portland, Me.....	1-3-1979	44
JOHN R. McKERNAN Jr.....	5-20-1948	Bangor, Me.......	1-8-1987	39

MAINE GUBERNATORIAL ELECTIONS

STATE OF MAINE

DATE	DEMOCRATIC VOTE		REPUBLICAN VOTE	
11-7-1978	J. BRENNAN......176,493	47.7%	L. Palmer Jr....126,862	34.2%
11-2-1982	J. BRENNAN......281,066	61.1%	C.R. Cragin.....172,949	37.6%
11-4-1986	J. Tierney......128,744	30.2%	J.R. McKERNAN...170,312	39.9%

PARTY	MAJOR OCCUPATIONS	MAINE RESIDENCE	DEATH DATE	AGE
Dem	lawyer...............	Augusta......................		
Rep	lawyer...............	Cumberland...................		

DATE	OTHER SIGNIFICANT VOTE	SCATTERED VOTE	
11-7-1978	H.Frankland.......I...65,889 17.8%	1,014	0.3%
11-2-1982	....	6,280	1.3%
11-4-1986	S.Huber...........I...64,317 15.1%	14	0.0%
	J.Menario.........I...63,474 14.8%		

I = Independent

MARYLAND GOVERNORS

STATE OF MARYLAND

GOVERNOR	BIRTH DATE	BIRTHPLACE	BECAME GOV.	AGE
HARRY ROE HUGHES........	11-13-1926	Easton, Md.......	1-17-1979	52
WILLIAM DONALD SCHAEFER.	11-2-1921	Baltimore, Md....	1-21-1987	65

MARYLAND GUBERNATORIAL ELECTIONS

STATE OF MARYLAND

DATE	DEMOCRATIC VOTE		REPUBLICAN VOTE	
11-7-1978	H.HUGHES........718,328	71.0%	J.Beall Jr......293,635	29.0%
11-2-1982	H.HUGHES........705,910	62.0%	R.Pascal........432,826	38.0%
11-4-1986	W.D.SCHAEFER....876,577	82.0%	T.J.Mooney......189,284	18.0%

PARTY	MAJOR OCCUPATIONS	MARYLAND RESIDENCE	DEATH DATE AGE
Dem	lawyer..............	Annapolis....................	
Dem	lawyer..............	Baltimore....................	

DATE	OTHER SIGNIFICANT VOTE	SCATTERED VOTE
11-7-1978	....	....
11-2-1982	....	....
11-4-1986	....	....

MASSACHUSETTS GOVERNORS

STATE OF MASSACHUSETTS

GOVERNOR	BIRTH DATE	BIRTHPLACE	BECAME GOV.	AGE
EDWARD J. KING..........	5-11-1925	Chelsea, Mass....	1-4-1979	53
MICHAEL S. DUKAKIS......	11-3-1933	Boston, Mass.....	1-6-1983	49

MASSACHUSETTS GUBERNATORIAL ELECTIONS

STATE OF MASSACHUSETTS

DATE	DEMOCRATIC VOTE		REPUBLICAN VOTE	
11-7-1978	E.KING........1,030,294	52.5%	F.Hatch Jr......926,072	47.2%
11-2-1982	M.DUKAKIS.....1,219,109	59.5%	J.W.Sears.......749,679	36.6%
11-4-1986	M.DUKAKIS.....1,157,786	68.7%	G.Kariotis......525,364	31.2%

PARTY	MAJOR OCCUPATIONS	MASSACHUSETTS RESIDENCE	DEATH DATE AGE
Dem	businessman..........	Winthrop.....................	
Dem	lawyer...............	Brookline...................	

DATE	OTHER SIGNIFICANT VOTE		SCATTERED VOTE	
11-7-1978	....	.....	5,885	0.3%
11-2-1982	....	.....	81,466	3.9%
11-4-1986	....	.....	929	0.1%

MICHIGAN GOVERNORS

STATE OF MICHIGAN

GOVERNOR	BIRTH DATE	BIRTHPLACE	BECAME GOV.	AGE
WILLIAM G. MILLIKEN.....	3-22-1922	Traverse City, Mich	1-1-1971	48
JAMES J. BLANCHARD......	8-8-1942	Detroit, Mich......	1-1-1983	40

MICHIGAN GUBERNATORIAL ELECTIONS

STATE OF MICHIGAN

DATE	DEMOCRATIC VOTE		REPUBLICAN VOTE	
11-7-1978	W.Fitzgerald..1,237,256	43.2%	W.MILLIKEN....1,628,485	56.8%
11-2-1982	J.J.BLANCHARD.1,561,291	51.4%	R.H.Headlee...1,369,582	45.1%
11-4-1986	J.J.BLANCHARD.1,632,138	68.1%	W.Lucas.........753,647	31.4%

PARTY	MAJOR OCCUPATIONS	MICHIGAN RESIDENCE	DEATH DATE	AGE
Rep	businessman..........	Traverse City...............		
Dem	lawyer...............	Pleasant Ridge..............		

DATE	OTHER SIGNIFICANT VOTE	SCATTERED VOTE	
11-7-1978	....	....	
11-2-1982	....	109,135	3.5%
11-4-1986	....	10,779	0.5%

MINNESOTA GOVERNORS

STATE OF MINNESOTA

GOVERNOR	BIRTH DATE	BIRTHPLACE	BECAME GOV.	AGE
ALBERT QUIE............	9-18-1923	Dennison, Minn...	1-1-1979	55
RUDY G. PERPICH........	6-27-1928	Carson Lake, Minn	1-3-1983	54

MINNESOTA GUBERNATORIAL ELECTIONS

STATE OF MINNESOTA

DATE	DEMOCRATIC VOTE	REPUBLICAN VOTE
11-7-1978	R.Perpich..DFL..718,244 45.3%	A.QUIE...IRP....830,019 52.3%
11-2-1982	R.PERPICH.DFL.1,049,104 58.8%	W.Whitney..IRP..711,796 39.9%
11-4-1986	R.PERPICH..DFL..790,138 56.1%	C.Ludeman..IRP..606,755 43.1%

DFL = Democratic-Farmer Labor   IR = Independent Republican

PARTY	MAJOR OCCUPATIONS	MINNESOTA RESIDENCE	DEATH DATE AGE
IRP	farmer...............	west of Dennison, Rice Co....	
DFL	dentist.............	Hibbing......................	

DFL = Democratic Farmer Labor   IRP = Independent Republican

DATE	OTHER SIGNIFICANT VOTE	SCATTERED VOTE	
11-7-1978	....	37,439	2.4%
11-2-1982	....	24,639	1.3%
11-4-1986	....	11,211	0.8%

MISSISSIPPI GOVERNORS

STATE OF MISSISSIPPI

GOVERNOR	BIRTH DATE	BIRTHPLACE	BECAME GOV.	AGE
(CHARLES) CLIFTON FINCH.	4-4-1927	Pope, Miss.......	1-20-1976	48
WILLIAM FORREST WINTER..	2-21-1923	Grenada Co, Miss.	1-22-1980	56
WILLIAM (BILL) ALLAIN...	2-14-1928	Washington, Miss.	1-10-1984	56
RAY MABUS..............	10-11-1949	Ackerman, Miss...	1-12-1988	38

MISSISSIPPI GUBERNATORIAL ELECTIONS

STATE OF MISSISSIPPI

DATE	DEMOCRATIC VOTE		REPUBLICAN VOTE	
11-4-1975	C.FINCH.........369,568	52.2%	G.Carmichael....319,632	45.1%
11-6-1979	W.WINTER........413,620	61.1%	G.Carmichael....263,702	38.9%
11-8-1983	W.ALLAIN........409,209	55.1%	L.Bramlett......288,764	38.9%
11-3-1987	R.MABUS.........385,689	53.4%	J.Reed..........336,006	46.6%

PARTY	MAJOR OCCUPATIONS	MISSISSIPPI RESIDENCE	DEATH DATE	AGE
Dem	lawyer...............	Batesville...................		
Dem	lawyer...............	Jackson.....................		
Dem	lawyer...............	Hinds Co...................		
Dem	lawyer, businessman..	Jackson.....................		

DATE	OTHER SIGNIFICANT VOTE	SCATTERED VOTE	
11-4-1975	....	18,833	2.7%
11-6-1979	....	....	
11-8-1983	J.C.Evers.........I....30,593 4.1%	14,171	1.9%
11-3-1987	....	....	

I = Independent

MISSOURI GOVERNORS

STATE OF MISSOURI

GOVERNOR	BIRTH DATE	BIRTHPLACE	BECAME GOV.	AGE
JOSEPH P. TEASDALE......	3-29-1936	Kansas City, Mo..	1-3-1977	40
CHRISTOPHER S. BOND.....	3-6-1939	St. Louis, Mo....	1-12-1981	41
JOHN DAVID ASHCROFT.....	5-9-1942	Chicago, Ill.....	1-14-1985	42

MISSOURI GUBERNATORIAL ELECTIONS

STATE OF MISSOURI

DATE	DEMOCRATIC VOTE		REPUBLICAN VOTE	
11-2-1976	J.TEASDALE......971,184	50.2%	C.Bond.........958,110	49.6%
11-4-1980	J.Teasdale......981,884	47.0%	C.BOND........1,098,950	52.6%
11-6-1984	K.Rothman.......913,700	43.3%	J.ASHCROFT....1,194,506	56.7%

PARTY	MAJOR OCCUPATIONS	MISSOURI RESIDENCE	DEATH DATE AGE
Dem	lawyer..............	Kansas City..................	
Rep	lawyer..............	Kansas City..................	
Rep	lawyer, professor....	Jefferson City..............	

DATE	OTHER SIGNIFICANT VOTE		SCATTERED VOTE	
11-2-1976	....	.....	4,281	0.2%
11-4-1980	....	.....	7,193	0.4%
11-6-1984	....	......	....	.....

MONTANA GOVERNORS

STATE OF MONTANA

GOVERNOR	BIRTH DATE	BIRTHPLACE	BECAME GOV.	AGE
THOMAS L. JUDGE.........	10-12-1934	Helena, Mont.....	1-1-1973	40
TED SCHWINDEN...........	8-31-1925	Wolf Point, Mont.	1-5-1981	55

MONTANA GUBERNATORIAL ELECTIONS

STATE OF MONTANA

DATE	DEMOCRATIC VOTE		REPUBLICAN VOTE	
11-2-1976	T.JUDGE.........195,420	61.7%	R.Woodahl.......115,848	36.6%
11-4-1980	T.SCHWINDEN.....199,574	55.4%	J.Ramirez.......160,892	44.6%
11-6-1984	T.SCHWINDEN.....266,578	70.3%	P.Goodover......100,070	26.4%

PARTY	MAJOR OCCUPATIONS	MONTANA RESIDENCE	DEATH DATE AGE
Dem	businessman..........	Helena......................	
Dem	grain farmer.........	Helena......................	

DATE	OTHER SIGNIFICANT VOTE		SCATTERED VOTE	
11-2-1976	....	.....	5,452	1.7%
11-4-1980	....	.....	....	.....
11-6-1984	....	.....	12,322	3.3%

NEBRASKA GOVERNORS

STATE OF NEBRASKA

GOVERNOR	BIRTH DATE	BIRTHPLACE	BECAME GOV.	AGE
CHARLES THONE...........	1-4-1924	Hartington, Neb..	1-4-1979	55
ROBERT KERREY...........	8-27-1943	Lincoln, Neb.....	1-6-1983	39
KAY (STARK) ORR.........	1-2-1939	Burlington, Iowa.	1-8-1987	48

NEBRASKA GUBERNATORIAL ELECTIONS

STATE OF NEBRASKA

DATE	DEMOCRATIC VOTE		REPUBLICAN VOTE	
11-7-1978	G.Whelan........216,754	44.0%	C.THONE.........275,473	56.0%
11-2-1982	R.KERREY........277,436	50.6%	C.Thone.........270,203	49.3%
11-4-1986	H.Boosalis......260,638	47.0%	K.A.ORR.........290,883	53.0%

PARTY	MAJOR OCCUPATIONS	NEBRASKA RESIDENCE	DEATH DATE AGE
Rep	lawyer..............	Lincoln......................	
Dem	pharmacist..........	Lincoln......................	
Rep	government service...	Lincoln......................	

DATE	OTHER SIGNIFICANT VOTE	SCATTERED VOTE	
11-7-1978	....	196	0.0%
11-2-1982	....	263	0.1%
11-4-1986	....	....	.....

NEVADA GOVERNORS

STATE OF NEVADA

GOVERNOR	BIRTH DATE	BIRTHPLACE	BECAME GOV.	AGE
ROBERT F. LIST..........	9-1-1936	Visalia, Cal.....	1-2-1979	42
RICHARD H. BRYAN........	7-16-1937	Washington, D.C..	1-3-1983	45

NEVADA GUBERNATORIAL ELECTIONS

STATE OF NEVADA

DATE	DEMOCRATIC VOTE		REPUBLICAN VOTE	
11-7-1978	R.Rose...........76,361	39.7%	R.LIST..........108,097	56.2%
11-2-1982	R.H.BRYAN.......128,132	53.4%	R.List..........100,104	41.8%
11-4-1986	R.H.BRYAN.......187,268	71.9%	P.Cafferata......65,081	25.0%

PARTY	MAJOR OCCUPATIONS	NEVADA RESIDENCE	DEATH DATE AGE
Rep	lawyer..............	Carson City..................	
Dem	lawyer..............	Carson City..................	

DATE	OTHER SIGNIFICANT VOTE	SCATTERED VOTE	
11-7-1978	....	7,987	4.1%
11-2-1982	....	11,515	4.8%
11-4-1986	....	8,026	3.1%

NEW HAMPSHIRE GOVERNORS

STATE OF NEW HAMPSHIRE

GOVERNOR	BIRTH DATE	BIRTHPLACE	BECAME GOV.	AGE
HUGH J. GALLEN.........a	11-30-1924	Portland, Ore....	1-3-1979	52
Vesta M. Roy-acting.....	3-36-1925	Detroit, Mich....	12-29-1982	57
JOHN H. SUNUNU..........	7-2-1939	Havana, Cuba.....	1-6-1983	43

a Died in office; succeeded by the Senate President

NEW HAMPSHIRE GUBERNATORIAL ELECTIONS

STATE OF NEW HAMPSHIRE

DATE	DEMOCRATIC VOTE		REPUBLICAN VOTE	
11-7-1978	H.GALLEN........133,133	49.4%	M.Thomson Jr....122,464	45.4%
11-4-1980	H.GALLEN........226,436	59.0%	M.Thomson Jr....156,178	40.7%
11-2-1982	H.Gallen........132,317	46.8%	J.H.SUNUNU......145,389	51.4%
11-6-1984	C.Spirou........127,156	33.1%	J.H.SUNUNU......256,574	66.9%
11-4-1986	P.McEachern.....116,154	46.0%	J.H.SUNUNU......134,674	54.0%

PARTY	MAJOR OCCUPATIONS	NEW HAMPSHIRE RESIDENCE	DEATH DATE	AGE
Dem	businessman..........	Littleton....................	12-29-1982	58
Rep	insurance agent......	Salem.......................		
Rep	engineer............	Salem.......................		

DATE	OTHER SIGNIFICANT VOTE		SCATTERED VOTE	
11-7-1978	W.Powell..........I...12,349	4.6%	1,641	0.6%
11-4-1980	....	.....	1,318	0.3%
11-2-1982	....	.....	4,785	0.8%
11-6-1984	....	.....	....	.....
11-4-1986	....	.....	....	.....

I = Independent

NEW JERSEY GOVERNORS

STATE OF NEW JERSEY

GOVERNOR	BIRTH DATE	BIRTHPLACE	BECAME GOV.	AGE
BRENDAN T. BYRNE........	4-1-1924	West Orange, N.J.	1-15-1974	49
THOMAS KEAN............	4-21-1935	New York, N.Y....	1-19-1982	46

NEW JERSEY GUBERNATORIAL ELECTIONS

STATE OF NEW JERSEY

DATE	DEMOCRATIC VOTE		REPUBLICAN VOTE	
11-8-1977	B.BYRNE.......1,184,564	55.7%	R.Bateman.......888,880	41.8%
11-3-1981	J.J.Florio....1,144,202	49.4%	T.H.KEAN......1,145,999	49.5%
11-5-1985	P.Shapiro.......578,402	29.6%	T.H.KEAN......1,372,631	70.4%

PARTY	MAJOR OCCUPATIONS	NEW JERSEY RESIDENCE	DEATH DATE AGE
Dem	lawyer, judge........	West Orange..................	
Rep	teacher, realtor.....	Livingston...................	

DATE	OTHER SIGNIFICANT VOTE		SCATTERED VOTE	
11-8-1977	....	.....	52,520	2.5%
11-3-1981	....	.....	27,038	1.1%
11-5-1985	....	......	....	.....

NEW MEXICO GOVERNORS

STATE OF NEW MEXICO

GOVERNOR	BIRTH DATE	BIRTHPLACE	BECAME GOV.	AGE
BRUCE KING..............	4-6-1924	Stanley, N.M.....	1-1-1979	54
TONEY ANAYA.............	4-29-1941	Moriarty, N.M....	1-1-1983	41
GARREY CARRUTHERS.......	8-29-1939	Aztec, N.M.......	1-1-1987	47

NEW MEXICO GUBERNATORIAL ELECTIONS

STATE OF NEW MEXICO

DATE	DEMOCRATIC VOTE		REPUBLICAN VOTE	
11-7-1978	B.KING..........174,631	50.5%	J.Skeen.........170,848	49.5%
11-2-1982	J.Irick.........191,626	47.0%	T.ANAYA.........215,840	53.0%
11-4-1986	R.B.Powell......179,748	47.0%	G.E.CARRUTHERS..203,640	53.0%

PARTY	MAJOR OCCUPATIONS	NEW MEXICO RESIDENCE	DEATH DATE AGE
Dem	rancher, businessman	nr. Stanley..................	
Dem	lawyer..............	Sante Fe.....................	
Rep	economist, professor.	Las Cruces..................	

DATE	OTHER SIGNIFICANT VOTE	SCATTERED VOTE
11-7-1978	....	....
11-2-1982	....	....
11-4-1986	....	....

NEW YORK GOVERNORS

STATE OF NEW YORK

GOVERNOR	BIRTH DATE	BIRTHPLACE	BECAME GOV.	AGE
HUGH L. CAREY...........	4-11-1919	Brooklyn, N.Y....	1-1-1975	55
MARIO MATTHEW CUOMO.....	6-15-1932	Queens, N.Y......	1-1-1983	50

NEW YORK GUBERNATORIAL ELECTIONS

STATE OF NEW YORK

DATE	DEMOCRATIC VOTE		REPUBLICAN VOTE	
11-7-1978	H.CAREY.......2,429,272	51.0%	P.Duryea......2,156,404	45.2%
11-2-1982	M.CUOMO..D-L..2,675,213	50.9%	L.Lehrman.C,SI2,494,827	47.5%
11-4-1986	M.CUOMO..D-L..2,775,229	64.6%	A.O'Rourke.C..1,363,810	31.8%

D = Democratic   R = Republican

L = Liberal   C = Conservative

SI = Statewide Independent

PARTY	MAJOR OCCUPATIONS	NEW YORK RESIDENCE	DEATH DATE AGE
Dem	lawyer..............	Brooklyn....................	
Dem	lawyer, professor....	Holliswood, Queens...........	

DATE	OTHER SIGNIFICANT VOTE		SCATTERED VOTE	
11-7-1978	....	.....	183,144	3.8%
11-2-1982	....	.....	84,665	1.6%
11-4-1986	....	.....	155,085	3.6%

NORTH CAROLINA GOVERNORS

STATE OF NORTH CAROLINA
_____

GOVERNOR	BIRTH DATE	BIRTHPLACE	BECAME GOV.	AGE
JAMES B. HUNT, Jr.......	5-16-1937	Greensboro, N.C..	1-6-1977	39
JAMES GRUBBS MARTIN.....	12-11-1935	Savannah, Ga.....	1-5-1985	49

NORTH CAROLINA GUBERNATORIAL ELECTIONS

STATE OF NORTH CAROLINA
_____

DATE	DEMOCRATIC VOTE		REPUBLICAN VOTE	
11-2-1976	J.HUNT Jr.....1,081,293	65.0%	D.Flaherty......564,102	33.9%
11-4-1980	J.HUNT Jr.....1,143,145	61.9%	B.Lake.........691,449	37.4%
11-6-1984	R.Edmisten....1,011,209	45.4%	J.G.MARTIN....1,208,167	54.3%

PARTY	MAJOR OCCUPATIONS	NORTH CAROLINA RESIDENCE	DEATH DATE AGE
Dem	lawyer, farmer.......	Raleigh.....................	
Rep	chemist, professor...	Lake Norman, Mooresville.....	

DATE	OTHER SIGNIFICANT VOTE		SCATTERED VOTE	
11-2-1976	....	.....	18,429	1.1%
11-4-1980	....	.....	12,838	0.7%
11-6-1984	....	.....	7,351	0.3%

NORTH DAKOTA GOVERNORS

STATE OF NORTH DAKOTA

GOVERNOR	BIRTH DATE	BIRTHPLACE	BECAME GOV.	AGE
ARTHUR A. LINK..........	5-24-1914	Alexander, N.D...	1-1-1973	58
ALLEN INGVAR OLSON......	11-5-1938	Rolla, N.D.......	1-6-1981	42
GEORGE SINNER...........	5-29-1928	Casselton, N.D...	1-8-1985	56

NORTH DAKOTA GUBERNATORIAL ELECTIONS

STATE OF NORTH DAKOTA

DATE	DEMOCRATIC VOTE		REPUBLICAN VOTE	
11-2-1976	A.LINK..........153,309	51.6%	R.Elkin........138,321	46.5%
11-4-1980	A.Link..........140,391	46.4%	A.OLSON.........162,230	53.6%
11-6-1984	G.SINNER........173,922	55.3%	A.Olson.........140,460	44.7%

PARTY	MAJOR OCCUPATIONS	NORTH DAKOTA RESIDENCE	DEATH DATE AGE
Dem	farmer...............	nr. Alexander................	
Rep	lawyer...............	Bismarck....................	
Dem	businessman..........	Casselton...................	

DATE	OTHER SIGNIFICANT VOTE		SCATTERED VOTE	
11-2-1976	....	.....	5,619	1.9%
11-4-1980	....	.....	....	.....
11-6-1984	....	.....	....	.....

OHIO GOVERNORS

STATE OF OHIO

GOVERNOR	BIRTH DATE	BIRTHPLACE	BECAME GOV.	AGE
JAMES A. RHODES.........	9-13-1909	Coalton, Ohio....	1-13-1975	65
RICHARD CELESTE.........	11-11-1937	Lakewood, Ohio...	1-10-1983	45

OHIO GUBERNATORIAL ELECTIONS

STATE OF OHIO

DATE	DEMOCRATIC VOTE		REPUBLICAN VOTE	
11-7-1978	R.Celeste.....1,354,631	47.6%	J.RHODES......1,402,167	49.3%
11-2-1982	R.CELESTE.....1,981,882	59.0%	C.J.Brown.....1,303,962	38.8%
11-4-1986	R.CELESTE.....1,858,372	60.6%	J.Rhodes......1,207,264	39.4%

PARTY	MAJOR OCCUPATIONS	OHIO RESIDENCE	DEATH DATE AGE
Rep	businessman.........	Columbus.....................	
Dem	real estate developer	Cleveland...................	

DATE	OTHER SIGNIFICANT VOTE	SCATTERED VOTE	
11-7-1978	....	86,553	3.1%
11-2-1982	....	70,884	2.2%
11-4-1986	....	975	0.0%

OKLAHOMA GOVERNORS

STATE OF OKLAHOMA

GOVERNOR	BIRTH DATE	BIRTHPLACE	BECAME GOV.	AGE
GEORGE PATTERSON NIGH..a	6-9-1927	McAlester, Okla..	1-3-1979	51
HENRY L. BELLMON........	9-3-1921	Tonkawa, Okla....	1-12-1987	65

a As lieutenant governor, succeeds to governorship upon resignation of
   Governor David Boren, Senator-elect. Term to which Nigh had been
   officially elected began 1-8-1979.

OKLAHOMA GUBERNATORIAL ELECTIONS

STATE OF OKLAHOMA

DATE	DEMOCRATIC VOTE		REPUBLICAN VOTE	
11-7-1978	G.NIGH.........402,240	51.7%	R.Shotts........367,055	47.2%
11-2-1982	G.NIGH.........548,159	62.1%	T.Daxon.........332,207	37.6%
11-4-1986	D.Walters.......405,295	44.5%	H.BELLMON.......431,762	47.5%

PARTY	MAJOR OCCUPATIONS	OKLAHOMA RESIDENCE	DEATH DATE AGE
Dem	teacher, grocer......	Oklahoma City...............	
Rep	farmer..............	Billings....................	

DATE	OTHER SIGNIFICANT VOTE		SCATTERED VOTE	
11-7-1978	....	.....	8,119	1.1%
11-2-1982	....	.....	2,764	0.3%
11-4-1986	J. Brown..........I...60,115	6.6%	12,753	1.4%

I = Independent

OREGON GOVERNORS

STATE OF OREGON

GOVERNOR	BIRTH DATE	BIRTHPLACE	BECAME GOV.	AGE
VICTOR G. ATIYEH........	2-20-1923	Portland, Ore....	1-8-1979	55
NEIL GOLDSCHMIDT........	6-16-1940	Eugene, Ore......	1-12-1987	46

OREGON GUBERNATORIAL ELECTIONS

STATE OF OREGON

DATE	DEMOCRATIC VOTE		REPUBLICAN VOTE	
11-7-1978	R.Straub........409,411	44.9%	V.ATIYEH........498,452	54.7%
11-2-1982	T.Kulongowski...374,316	35.9%	V.ATIYEH........639,841	61.4%
11-4-1986	N.GOLDSCHMIDT...518,490	52.0%	N.Paulus........472,954	48.0%

PARTY	MAJOR OCCUPATIONS	OREGON RESIDENCE	DEATH DATE AGE
Rep	businessman..........	Salem........................	
Dem	lawyer...............	Portland.....................	

DATE	OTHER SIGNIFICANT VOTE		SCATTERED VOTE	
11-7-1978	....	.....	3,280	0.4%
11-2-1982	....	.....	27,852	2.7%
11-4-1986	....	......	....	.....

PENNSYLVANIA GOVERNORS

STATE OF PENNSYLVANIA

GOVERNOR	BIRTH DATE	BIRTHPLACE	BECAME GOV.	AGE
RICHARD L. THORNBURGH...	7-16-1932	Pittsburgh, Pa...	1-16-1979	46
ROBERT PATRICK CASEY....	1-9-1932	Jackson Hghts.,NY	1-20-1987	55

PENNSYLVANIA GUBERNATORIAL ELECTIONS

STATE OF PENNSYLVANIA

DATE	DEMOCRATIC VOTE		REPUBLICAN VOTE	
11-7-1978	P.Flaherty....1,737,888	46.5%	R.THORNBURGH..1,966,042	52.5%
11-2-1982	A.Ertel.......1,772,353	48.1%	R.THORNBURGH..1,872,784	50.8%
11-4-1986	R.CASEY.......1,717,484	50.7%	W.Scranton....1,638,268	48.4%

PARTY	MAJOR OCCUPATIONS	PENNSYLVANIA RESIDENCE	DEATH DATE AGE
Rep	lawyer...............	Harrisburg...................	
Dem	lawyer...............	Scranton....................	

DATE	OTHER SIGNIFICANT VOTE		SCATTERED VOTE	
11-7-1978	....	.....	38,039	1.0%
11-2-1982	....	.....	38,848	1.1%
11-4-1986	....	.....	32,523	0.9%

RHODE ISLAND GOVERNORS

STATE OF RHODE ISLAND

GOVERNOR	BIRTH DATE	BIRTHPLACE	BECAME GOV.	AGE
JOHN JOSEPH GARRAHY.....	11-26-1930	Providence, R.I..	1-4-1977	46
EDWARD D. DiPRETE.......	7-8-1934	Cranston, R.I....	1-1-1985	50

RHODE ISLAND GUBERNATORIAL ELECTIONS

STATE OF RHODE ISLAND

DATE	DEMOCRATIC VOTE		REPUBLICAN VOTE	
11-7-1978	J.GARRAHY.......197,386	62.8%	L.Almond.........96,596	30.7%
11-4-1980	J.GARRAHY.......299,174	73.7%	V.Cianci........106,729	26.3%
11-2-1982	J.GARRAHY.......247,208	73.3%	V.Marzullo.......79,602	23.6%
11-6-1984	A.Solomon.......163,311	40.0%	E.DiPRETE.......245,059	60.0%
11-4-1986	B.Sundlun.......104,504	32.4%	E.DiPRETE.......208,822	64.7%

PARTY	MAJOR OCCUPATIONS	RHODE ISLAND RESIDENCE	DEATH DATE AGE
Dem	salesman............	Providence...................	
Rep	insurance agent......	Cranston....................	

DATE	OTHER SIGNIFICANT VOTE		SCATTERED VOTE	
11-7-1978	J.Doorley.........I...20,381	6.5%	18	0.0%
11-4-1980	....	.....	....	.....
11-2-1982	....	.....	10,438	3.1%
11-6-1984	....	.....	....	.....
11-4-1986	....	.....	9,445	2.9%

I = Independent

SOUTH CAROLINA GOVERNORS

STATE OF SOUTH CAROLINA

GOVERNOR	BIRTH DATE	BIRTHPLACE	BECAME GOV.	AGE
RICHARD W. RILEY........	1-2-1933	Greenville, S.C..	1-10-1979	46
CARROLL A. CAMPBELL, Jr.	7-24-1940	Greenville, S.C..	1-14-1987	46

SOUTH CAROLINA GUBERNATORIAL ELECTIONS

STATE OF SOUTH CAROLINA

DATE	DEMOCRATIC VOTE		REPUBLICAN VOTE	
11-7-1978	R.RILEY........385,016	61.4%	E.Young.........236,946	37.8%
11-2-1982	R.RILEY........468,819	69.8%	W.Workman Jr....202,806	30.2%
11-4-1986	M.Daniel.......361,325	47.9%	C.CAMPBELL Jr...384,565	51.0%

PARTY	MAJOR OCCUPATIONS	SOUTH CAROLINA RESIDENCE	DEATH DATE	AGE
Dem	lawyer..............	Columbia.....................		
Rep	horse breeder,realtor	Greenville...................		

DATE	OTHER SIGNIFICANT VOTE		SCATTERED VOTE	
11-7-1978	....	.....	5,338	0.8%
11-2-1982	....	.....	....	.....
11-4-1986	....	.....	7,861	1.1%

SOUTH DAKOTA GOVERNORS

STATE OF SOUTH DAKOTA

GOVERNOR	BIRTH DATE	BIRTHPLACE	BECAME GOV.	AGE
WILLIAM J. JANKLOW......	9-13-1939	Chicago, Ill.....	1-1-1979	39
GEORGE S. MICKELSEN.....	1-31-1941	Mobridge, S.D....	1-10-1987	46

SOUTH DAKOTA GUBERNATORIAL ELECTIONS

STATE OF SOUTH DAKOTA

DATE	DEMOCRATIC VOTE		REPUBLICAN VOTE	
11-7-1978	R.McKellips.....112,679	43.3%	W.JANKLOW.......147,116	56.7%
11-2-1982	M.O'Connor.......81,136	29.1%	W.JANKLOW.......197,426	70.9%
11-4-1986	R.L.Herseth.....140,566	48.0%	G.MICKELSEN.....150,416	52.0%

PARTY	MAJOR OCCUPATIONS	SOUTH DAKOTA RESIDENCE	DEATH DATE	AGE
Rep	lawyer...............	Pierre........................		
Rep	lawyer...............	Brookings.....................		

DATE	OTHER SIGNIFICANT VOTE		SCATTERED VOTE	
11-7-1978	....	.....	....	.....
11-2-1982	....	.....	....	.....
11-4-1986	....	.....	....	.....

TENNESSEE GOVERNORS

STATE OF TENNESSEE

GOVERNOR	BIRTH DATE	BIRTHPLACE	BECAME GOV.	AGE
LAMAR ALEXANDER.........	7-3-1940	Maryville, Tenn..	1-17-1979	38
NED McWHERTER..........	10-15-1930	Palmersville,Tenn	1-17-1987	56

TENNESSEE GUBERNATORIAL ELECTIONS

STATE OF TENNESSEE

DATE	DEMOCRATIC VOTE		REPUBLICAN VOTE	
11-7-1978	J.Butcher.......523,495	44.0%	L.ALEXANDER.....661,959	55.6%
11-2-1982	R.Tyree.........500,937	40.4%	L.ALEXANDER.....737,963	59.6%
11-4-1986	N.McWHERTER.....657,426	54.0%	W.Dunn..........552,900	46.0%

PARTY	MAJOR OCCUPATIONS	TENNESSEE RESIDENCE	DEATH DATE	AGE
Rep	reporter, lawyer.....	Nashville....................		
Dem	farmer, businessman..	Dresden.....................		

DATE	OTHER SIGNIFICANT VOTE		SCATTERED VOTE	
11-7-1978	....	.....	4,241	0.4%
11-2-1982	....	.....	....	.....
11-4-1986	....	.....	....	.....

TEXAS GOVERNORS

STATE OF TEXAS

GOVERNOR	BIRTH DATE	BIRTHPLACE	BECAME GOV.	AGE
WILLIAM P. CLEMENTS, Jr.	4-13-1917	Dallas, Tex......	1-16-1979	61
MARK WHITE..............	3-17-1940	Henderson, Tex...	1-18-1983	42
WILLIAM P. CLEMENTS, Jr.	4-13-1917	Dallas, Tex......	1-20-1987	69

TEXAS GUBERNATORIAL ELECTIONS

STATE OF TEXAS

DATE	DEMOCRATIC VOTE	REPUBLICAN VOTE
11-7-1978	J.Hill........1,166,979 49.3%	W.CLEMENTS Jr.1,183,839 49.9%
11-2-1982	M.WHITE Jr....1,697,870 53.2%	W.Clements Jr.1,465,937 45.9%
11-4-1986	M.White Jr....1,584,515 46.0%	W.CLEMENTS Jr.1,813,779 52.7%

PARTY	MAJOR OCCUPATIONS	TEXAS RESIDENCE	DEATH DATE	AGE
Rep	oilman..............	Dallas......................		
Dem	lawyer..............	Austin......................		
Rep	oilman..............	Dallas......................		

DATE	OTHER SIGNIFICANT VOTE		SCATTERED VOTE	
11-7-1978	....	.....	18,946	0.8%
11-2-1982	....	.....	27,284	0.9%
11-4-1986	....	.....	43,166	1.3%

UTAH GOVERNORS

STATE OF UTAH

GOVERNOR	BIRTH DATE	BIRTHPLACE	BECAME GOV.	AGE
SCOTT M. MATHESON.......	1-8-1929	Chicago, Ill.....	1-3-1977	47
NORMAN H. BANGERTER.....	1-4-1933	Granger, Utah....	1-7-1985	52

UTAH GUBERNATORIAL ELECTIONS

STATE OF UTAH

DATE	DEMOCRATIC VOTE		REPUBLICAN VOTE	
11-2-1976	S.MATHESON......280,706	52.0%	V.Romney........248,027	46.0%
11-4-1980	S.MATHESON......330,974	55.2%	R.Wright........266,578	44.4%
11-6-1984	W.Owens.........275,669	43.8%	N.BANGERTER.....351,792	55.9%

PARTY	MAJOR OCCUPATIONS	UTAH RESIDENCE	DEATH DATE	AGE
Dem	lawyer...............	Salt Lake City...............		
Rep	real estate developer	Salt Lake City...............		

DATE	OTHER SIGNIFICANT VOTE		SCATTERED VOTE	
11-2-1976	....	.....	10,916	2.0%
11-4-1980	....	.....	2,467	0.4%
11-6-1984	....	.....	2,158	0.3%

VERMONT GOVERNORS

STATE OF VERMONT
_____

GOVERNOR	BIRTH DATE	BIRTHPLACE	BECAME GOV.	AGE
RICHARD A. SNELLING.....	2-18-1927	Allentown, Pa....	1-5-1977	49
MADELEINE MAY KUNIN.....	9-28-1933	Zurich, Swit.....	1-10-1985	51

VERMONT GUBERNATORIAL ELECTIONS

STATE OF VERMONT
_____

DATE	DEMOCRATIC VOTE		REPUBLICAN VOTE	
11-7-1978	E.Granai.........42,482	34.1%	R.SNELLING.......78,181	62.8%
11-4-1980	M.J.Diamond......76,826	36.6%	R.SNELLING......123,229	58.7%
11-2-1982	M.M.Kunin........74,394	44.0%	R.SNELLING.......93,111	55.0%
11-6-1984	M.M.KUNIN.......116,938	50.0%	J.J.Easton Jr...113,264	48.5%
11-4-1986	M.M.KUNIN........92,485	47.0%	P.Smith..........75,239	38.2%

PARTY	MAJOR OCCUPATIONS	VERMONT RESIDENCE	DEATH DATE AGE
Rep	businessman.........	Shelburne....................	
Dem	journalist, writer...	Burlington...................	

DATE	OTHER SIGNIFICANT VOTE		SCATTERED VOTE	
11-7-1978	....	.....	3,819	3.1%
11-4-1980	....	.....	9,789	4.7%
11-2-1982	....	.....	1,746	1.0%
11-6-1984	....	.....	3,551	1.5%
11-4-1986	B.Sanders.........I...28,418	14.4%	574	0.4%

VIRGINIA GOVERNORS

STATE OF VIRGINIA

GOVERNOR	BIRTH DATE	BIRTHPLACE	BECAME GOV.	AGE
JOHN N. DALTON..........	7-11-1931	Emporia, Va......	1-14-1978	46
CHARLES ROBB............	6-26-1939	Phoenix, Ariz....	1-16-1982	42
GERALD L. BALILES.......	7-8-1940	Patrick Co, Va...	1-11-1986	45

VIRGINIA GUBERNATORIAL ELECTIONS

STATE OF VIRGINIA

DATE	DEMOCRATIC VOTE		REPUBLICAN VOTE	
11-8-1977	H.Howell........541,319	43.3%	J.DALTON........699,302	55.9%
11-3-1981	C.ROBB..........760,357	53.5%	J.M.Coleman.....659,398	46.4%
11-5-1985	G.L.BALILES.....741,438	55.2%	W.B.Durrette....601,652	44.8%

PARTY	MAJOR OCCUPATIONS	VIRGINIA RESIDENCE	DEATH DATE	AGE
Rep	businessman..........	Radford......................	7-30-1986	55
Dem	lawyer...............	McLean......................		
Dem	lawyer...............	Richmond....................		

DATE	OTHER SIGNIFICANT VOTE	SCATTERED VOTE	
11-8-1977	....	10,101	0.8%
11-3-1981	....	856	0.1%
11-5-1985	....	....	.....

WASHINGTON GOVERNORS

STATE OF WASHINGTON

GOVERNOR	BIRTH DATE	BIRTHPLACE	BECAME GOV.	AGE
DIXY LEE RAY............	9-3-1914	Tacoma, Wash.....	1-10-1977	62
JOHN SPELLMAN...........	12-29-1926	Seattle, Wash....	1-14-1981	54
BOOTH GARDNER...........	8-21-1936	Tacoma, Wash.....	1-16-1985	48

WASHINGTON GUBERNATORIAL ELECTIONS

STATE OF WASHINGTON

DATE	DEMOCRATIC VOTE		REPUBLICAN VOTE	
11-2-1976	D.RAY..........821,797	53.1%	J.Spellman......687,039	44.5%
11-4-1980	J.McDermott.....749,813	43.3%	J.SPELLMAN......981,083	56.7%
11-6-1984	B.GARDNER....1,006,993	53.3%	J.Spellman......881,994	46.7%

PARTY	MAJOR OCCUPATIONS	WASHINGTON RESIDENCE	DEATH DATE	AGE
Dem	scientist, educator..	Fox Island....................		
Rep	lawyer..............	King Co......................		
Dem	lumber executive.....	Tacoma.......................		

DATE	OTHER SIGNIFICANT VOTE		SCATTERED VOTE	
11-2-1976	....	.....	37,546	2.4%
11-4-1980	....	.....	....	.....
11-6-1984	....	.....	....	.....

WEST VIRGINIA GOVERNORS

STATE OF WEST VIRGINIA

GOVERNOR	BIRTH DATE	BIRTHPLACE	BECAME GOV.	AGE
JOHN D. ROCKEFELLER 4th.	6-18-1937	New York, N.Y....	1-17-1977	39
ARCH A. MOORE Jr........	4-16-1923	Moundsville, W Va	1-14-1985	61

WEST VIRGINIA GUBERNATORIAL ELECTIONS

STATE OF WEST VIRGINIA

DATE	DEMOCRATIC VOTE		REPUBLICAN VOTE	
11-2-1976	J.ROCKEFELLER...495,661	66.2%	C.Underwood.....253,420	33.8%
11-4-1980	J.ROCKEFELLER...401,863	54.1%	A.Moore Jr......337,240	45.4%
11-6-1984	C.M.See Jr......346,565	46.7%	A.MOORE Jr......394,937	53.3%

PARTY	MAJOR OCCUPATIONS	WEST VIRGINIA RESIDENCE	DEATH DATE AGE
Dem	government service...	Charleston..................	
Rep	lawyer..............	Glendall...................	

DATE	OTHER SIGNIFICANT VOTE		SCATTERED VOTE	
11-2-1976	....	.....	189	0.0%
11-4-1980	....	.....	3,047	0.5%
11-6-1984	....	......	....	.....

WISCONSIN GOVERNORS

STATE OF WISCONSIN

GOVERNOR	BIRTH DATE	BIRTHPLACE	BECAME GOV.	AGE
LEE S. DREYFUS..........	6-20-1926	Milwaukee, Wis...	1-1-1979	52
ANTHONY S. EARL.........	4-12-1936	Lansing, Mich....	1-3-1983	46
TOMMY G. THOMPSON.......	11-19-1941	Elroy, Wis.......	1-5-1987	45

WISCONSIN GUBERNATORIAL ELECTIONS

STATE OF WISCONSIN

DATE	DEMOCRATIC VOTE		REPUBLICAN VOTE	
11-7-1978	M.Schreiber.....673,813	44.9%	L.DREYFUS.......816,056	54.4%
11-2-1982	A.S.EARL........896,812	56.7%	T.J.Kohler......662,838	41.9%
11-4-1986	A.S.Earl........705,578	46.2%	T.G.THOMPSON....805,090	52.7%

PARTY	MAJOR OCCUPATIONS	WISCONSIN RESIDENCE	DEATH DATE AGE
Rep	businessman,educator.	Stevens Point...............	
Dem	lawyer..............	Madison.....................	
Rep	lawyer, realtor......	Elroy.......................	

DATE	OTHER SIGNIFICANT VOTE	SCATTERED VOTE	
11-7-1978	....	10,935	0.7%
11-2-1982	....	20,694	1.4%
11-4-1986	....	16,292	1.1%

WYOMING GOVERNORS

STATE OF WYOMING

GOVERNOR	BIRTH DATE	BIRTHPLACE	BECAME GOV.	AGE
EDGAR J. HERSCHLER......	10-27-1918	Kemmerer, Wyo....	1-6-1975	56
MIKE SULLIVAN...........	9-22-1939	Omaha, Neb.......	1-5-1987	47

WYOMING GUBERNATORIAL ELECTIONS

STATE OF WYOMING

DATE	DEMOCRATIC VOTE		REPUBLICAN VOTE	
11-7-1978	E.HERSCHLER......69,972	50.9%	J.Ostlund........67,595	49.1%
11-2-1982	E.HERSCHLER.....106,427	63.1%	W.Morton.........62,128	36.9%
11-4-1986	M.SULLIVAN.......88,827	54.0%	P.Simpson........75,775	46.0%

PARTY	MAJOR OCCUPATIONS	WYOMING RESIDENCE	DEATH DATE AGE
Dem	lawyer..............	Kemmerer.....................	
Dem	lawyer..............	Cheyenne.....................	

DATE	OTHER SIGNIFICANT VOTE		SCATTERED VOTE	
11-7-1978	....	.....	....	.....
11-2-1982	....	.....	....	.....
11-4-1986	....	.....	....	.....

Bibliographic Note

Basic biographical information about various state political officials, including governors, is catalogued in *Who's Who in American Politics,* edited by Jaques Cattell Press (New York: R.R. Bowker) 6th-10th eds., 1977-1985. Capsule biographies of American governors are prepared and compiled on a regular basis by the National Governors Association, Hall of the States, 444 North Capitol Street, Washington, D. C. 20001. Their most recent publication is *Governors of the American States, Commonwealths, and Territories: Biographical Sketches and Portraits,* 1986. Also see Meckler's *Biographical Directory of the Governors of the United States, 1789-1978,* edited by Robert Sobel and John W. Raimo, and *Biographical Directory of Governors of the United States, 1978-1983,* edited by John W. Raimo. An updated edition, 1983-1988, is forthcoming. More detailed biographical information, including a summary of each governor's legislative achievements and programs, can usually be obtained directly from the Governor's Office or Governor's Press Secretary in each state.

Congressional Quarterly, an editorial research service and publishing company, publishes a *Weekly Report* on state and national political developments, including election statistics. These have been compiled in Congressional Quarterly's *Guide to U.S. Elections,* 2nd ed. (Washington D.C.: Congressional Quarterly, 1985). The national headquarters for statistical information on election returns and voting behavior is the Elections Research Center, 1321 Connecticut Avenue N.W., Washington, D.C. 20036. Annually, the Elections Research Center publishes *America Votes: A Handbook of Contemporary American Election Statistics,* edited by Richard M. Scammon and Alice V. McGillivray. The most direct and complete source of voting records and statisitics remains the offices of the Secretary of State in each of the 50 states, charged officially with keeping such data, publishing it on a regular basis, and making it available to the public.

Each state also publishes, on an annual or biennial basis, an offical state legislative manual, containing much valuable information about state political leaders and legislative issues. Michael Barone's *The Almanac of American Politics,* published in even-number years by the National Journal, Washington, D.C., contains a wealth of detailed information and political commentary and analysis about state politics and personalities.